English

Like

Butter

A step by step guide to Spoken English

About the Book

After years of teaching students from different parts of the world, this book has been compiled. It aims at only one thing, to help students to communicate in English. The contents are based on conversational English, if anyone desires to study English grammar in depth; other books are to be used. This book is especially for those who know how to read English but find it difficult to communicate. It is a great book for Beginners; it will show them how easy it is to speak.

Contents

Chapter 1

AM, Is ,Are – we use this to talk about present emotions/descriptions or action happening now.

Use "am" with I	I am = I'm
Use "is" with he/she/it	He is = he's She is = she's It is = It's
Use "are" with we/you/they	We are = we're You are = You're They are = They're

For Possession meaning belonging to we use
my,our,your,his,her,their

My +   noun/nouns
Our + noun/nouns
Your + noun/nouns
His + noun/nouns
Her + noun/nouns
Their + noun/nouns

Examples:-
- My book/books
- Our money
- Your brother/brothers
- His sister/sisters

- **Adjective – is a word that describes a noun like size,shape,color,age etc.**

Examples

1.	Basic	26.	Polite	51.	Brave
2.	Advanced	27.	Shy	52.	Depressed
3.	Good	28.	Proud	53.	Confused
4.	Bad	29.	Cruel	54.	Embarrassed
5.	Better	30.	Naughty	55.	Ashamed
6.	Fat	31.	Upset	56.	Guilty
7.	Slim	32.	Anxious	57.	Innocent
8.	Slow	33.	Curious	58.	Surprised
9.	Fast	34.	Nervous	59.	Shocked
10.	Big	35.	Boring	60.	Ambitious
11.	Small	36.	Bored	61.	Generous
12.	Tiny	37.	Exciting	62.	Mean
13.	Cold	38.	Excited	63.	Kind
14.	Warm	39.	Interesting	64.	Selfish
15.	Hot	40.	Interested	65.	Impatient
16.	Tall	41.	Smart	66.	Patient
17.	Short	42.	Stupid	67.	Aggressive
18.	Long	43.	Genius	68.	Humble
19.	Heavy	44.	Respected	69.	Responsible
20.	Light	45.	Disappointed	70.	Irresponsible
21.	Afraid	46.	Fed up	71.	Honest
22.	Scared	47.	Exhausted	72.	Dishonest
23.	Confident	48.	Tired	73.	Strict
24.	Hungry	49.	Frustrated	74.	Lenient
25.	Angry	50.	Efficient	75.	Funny

I am + Adjective

He is + Adjective
She is + Adjective
It is + Adjective

We are + Adjective
You are + Adjective
They are + Adjective

Examples

- I am excited
- He is cruel
- She is tall
- We are bored
- You are nervous
- They are polite

Exercise

- I am ………………………..

- He is ………………………

- She is ………………….…...

- We are ……………………...

- You are ……………………

- They are ……………………

3

Verb with – "ing"

When we use verbs with "ing" ending we mean to say it is a continuous action. Examples eat,sleep,drink,walk etc.. we add "ing" to the end of the verbs

Eat = eating

Sleep = sleeping

Drink = drinking

1.	Get
2.	See
3.	Need
4.	Know
5.	Find
6.	Take
7.	Want
8.	Learn
9.	Become
10.	Come
11.	Include
12.	Thank
13.	Provide
14.	Create
15.	Add
16.	Understand
17.	Consider
18.	Choose
19.	Develop
20.	Remember
21.	Determine
22.	Grow

23. Allow
24. Supply
25. Bring
26. Improve
27. Maintain
28. Begin
29. Exist
30. Tend

Some verbs cannot end in "ing"

agree, be, believe, belong, contain, cost, depend, expect, feel, forget, hate, hear, hope, imagin, know, like, look, love, matter, mean, need, notice, own, prefer, realise, recognise, remember, see, seem, smell, suppose, taste, think, understand, want, wish

I am+ verb-"ing"

He is+ verb-"ing"
She is+ verb-"ing"
It is+ verb-"ing"

We are+ verb-"ing"
You are+ verb-"ing"
They are+ verb-"ing"

Examples

- I am reading a book
- He is washing his plate
- She is cooking
- We are studying
- You are playing
- They are walking

Exercise

- I am ....
- He is ....
- She is ....
- We are ....
- You are ....
- They are ....

Preposition – is a word that shows the relationship between two other nearby words.

Examples – in ,at from,on etc…

On	Days	On Monday
	A surface	On the table
	Side	On the left
	Floor	On the first floor
	Vehicles	On the bus
	T.V/Radio	On T.V
In	Months/seasons	In june/in winter
At	Night	At night
	Weekend	At the weekend
	A certain point of time	At midnight
Ago	Time in the past	2 days/years ago
Before	Earlier than a certain time	Before 2004
In	Room/building/country etc	In the kitchen/class
	Book/paper	In the book
	Car /taxi	In a taxi
At	Next to	At the door
	Table	At the table
	Events	At the party
	Place	At school/work
	Age	At 16
By	Around	By 10 o' clock
	Means of transportation	By bus
	Person	By the president

		Next to	By the car
Through		Something	Drive through the tunnel
		Person	Through him
To		Person/building	To him/school
		Place	To UAE
From		Place	From Mumbai
		Person	From my teacher
About		Something	About food
		Person	About the president

Here we will use in,at,from,on

I am + preposition + noun

He is+ preposition + noun
She is+ preposition + noun
It is+ preposition + noun

We are+ preposition + noun
You are+ preposition + noun
They are+ preposition + noun

Examples

- I am at home
- He is in class
- She is in the car
- It is on the table
- We are from Australia
- You are in a problem
- They are at the bus stop

Exercise

- I am ....

- He is ....

- She is ....

- It is ....

- We are ....

- You are ....

- They are ....

Noun – can be the name of a person, place or thing. Here we will use for name of the person and for job titles . example – doctor, teacher etc…

I am+ noun (name/job)

He is + noun (name/job)
She is + noun (name/job)
It is + noun (name/job)
We are+ noun (name/job)
You are+ noun (name/job)
They are + noun (name/job)

Examples

- I am Harry
- He is a doctor
- She is a teacher
- It is a book

(we can use only name of a thing with "It")

When we use a singular noun we use "a" or "an". With nouns beginning with vowels we use "an". With plural nouns "a" & "an" are not used.

- We are trainers
- They are consultants

Exercise

- I am ……………………………………
- He is ……………………………………..
- She is ……………………………………
- It is ……………………………………
- We are ……………………………………
- They are ……………………………………

Negative – using "not"

I am not = I'm not

He is not = He's not / He isn't

She is not = She's not /She isn't

It is not = It's not / It isn't

We are not = we're not / we aren't

You are not = you're not/ you aren't

They are not = They're not/ they aren't

Adjective

I am not + adjective

He is not + adjective
She is not + adjective
It is not + adjective

We are not + adjective
You are not + adjective
They are not + adjective

Examples

- I am not excited / I'm not excited

- He is not cruel / He's not cruel /He isn't cruel

- She is not tall   / she's not tall / she isn't tall

- We are not bored / we're not bored / we aren't bored

- You are not nervous / you're not nervous / you aren't nervous

- They are not polite / they 're not polite / they aren't polite

Exercise

- I am not ....

- He is not ....

- She is not ....

- We are not ....

- You are not ....

- They are not ....

Verb

I am not + verb –ing

He is not + verb –ing
She is not + verb –ing
It is not + verb –ing
We are not + verb –ing
You are not + verb –ing
They are not + verb –ing

Examples

- I am not reading a book/ I'm not reading

- He is not washing his plate/ He's not washing his plate

- She is not cooking/ she's not cooking

- We are not studying / We're not studying

- You are not playing / you're not playing

- They are not walking/ They're not walking

Exercise

- I am ………………………………...
- He is ………………………………
- She is ………………………………
- We are ………………………………..
- You are ………………………………
- They are ………………………………

Preposition

I am not + preposition + noun

He is not + preposition + noun
She is not + preposition + noun
It is not + preposition + noun

We are not + preposition + noun
You are not + preposition + noun
They are not + preposition + noun

Examples

- I am not at home / I'm not at home

- He is not in class/ He's not in class

- She is not in the car/ she's not in the car

- It is not on the table/ It's not on the table

- We are not from Australia/ we're not from Australia

- You are not in a problem/ you're not in a problem

Exercise

- I am ………………………………
- He is ………………………………..
- She is ………………………………
- It is ………………………………
- We are ………………………………
- You are ………………………………..

Noun

I am not + noun(name/job)

He is not + noun(name/job)
She is not + noun(name/job)
It is not + noun(name/job)

We are not + noun(name/job)
You are not + noun(name/job)
They are not + noun(name/job)

Examples

- I am not Harry/ I'm not Harry
- He is not a doctor/ He's not a doctor
- She is not a Teacher / She's not a Teacher
- It is not a book/ It's not a book
- We are not Trainers/ We're not Trainers
- They are not consultants/ They're not consultants

Exercise

- I am not ………………………………….

- He is not ………………………………….

- She is not ………………………………….

- It is not …………………………………..

- We are not…………………………………..

- They are ………………………………….

15

Questions

Adjective

Am I + adjective ?

Is he + adjective ?
Is she+ adjective?
Is it + adjective ?

Are we+ adjective ?
Are you+ adjective ?
Are they + adjective ?

In casual conversations grammatical answers are rarely used. More of informal answers are used by many, here we will see casual conversational answers.

Examples

- Am I late?

Answer;- you are late / you are not late

- Is he famous?

Answer;- he is famous/ he is not famous

- Is she angry?

Answer: - She is angry /she is not angry

- Are we stuck?

Answer:- we are stuck/ we are not stuck

- Are you ready?

Answer:- I am ready/ I am not ready

- Are they honest?

Answer:- They are honest/They are not honest

Exercise

- Am I ………………….?
- Is he ………………….?
- Is she ……………………?
- Are we …………………..?
- Are you …………………..?
- Are they …………………….?

Verb

Am I+ verb - ing?

Is he + verb - ing?
Is she + verb - ing?
Is it + verb - ing?

Are we + verb - ing?
Are you + verb - ing?
Are they + verb - ing?

Examples

- Am I disturbing you ?

Answer:- you are disturbing me/you are not disturbing
- Is he improving?

Answer :- He is improving/He is not improving
- Is it raining ?

Answer :- It is raining /it is not raining
- Are we taking this?

Answer:- we are taking this / we are not taking this
- Are you making tea?

Answer:- I am making tea/ I am not making tea

Exercise

- Am I ....?

- Is he ....?

- Is it ....?

- Are we ....?

- Are you ....?

- Are they ....?

Preposition

Am I + preposition + noun?

Is he + preposition + noun?
Is she + preposition + noun?
Is it + preposition + noun?

Are we + preposition + noun?
Are you + preposition + noun?
Are they + preposition + noun?

Examples

- Is he at home?

Answer :- He is at home/He is not at home

- Is she in a problem?

Answer:- She is in a big problem /she is not in a problem

- Are we at the right place?

Answer:- we are at the right place/We are not at the right place

- Are you from Australia?

Answer:- I am from Australia/I am not from Australia

- Are they in the car?

Answer:- They are in the car/They are not in the car

Exercise

- Is he ....?

- Is she ....?

- Are we ....?

- Are you ....?

- Are they ....?

Noun

Is he + noun?
Is she + noun?
Is it + noun?

Are you + noun/nouns?
Are they + nouns?

Examples

- Is he a doctor?

Answer:- He is a doctor/He is not a Doctor
- Is she a Teacher?

Answer:- She is a Teacher /She is not a Teacher
- Is it a pen?

Answer:- It is a pen/It is not a pen
- Are you a Builder?

Answer:- I am a Builder/I am not a Builder
- Are they painters?

Answer:- They are painters/They are not Painters
   Exercise

- Is he …………………………..?

- Is she ………………………..?

- Is it …………………………....?

- Are you ……………………….?

- Are they ……………………….?

Wh- Questions

Verb

What is he/she + verb-ing?

Where is he/she + verb-ing?

When is he/she + verb-ing?

Why is he/she + verb-ing?

How is he/she + verb-ing?

Examples

- What is he eating?

Answer:- He is eating fruits

- Where is she going ?

Answer:- She is going to class

- When is he coming ?

Answer:- He is coming now

- Why is she crying?

Answer:- She is sad (it is not necessary that we use –ing form for answers always)

- How is he coming ?

Answer:- He is coming by car

Exercise

What is he ....?

Where is she ....?

When is he ....?

Why is she ....?

How is he ....?

What are we/you/they + verb-ing?
Where are we/you/they + verb-ing?
When are we/you/they + verb-ing?
Why are we/you/they + verb-ing?
How are we/you/they + verb-ing?

Examples

- What are you doing?

Answer:- I am reading a book

- Where are they going?

Answer:- They are going home

- When are we meeting him?

Answer:- He is coming now

- Why are you running?

Answer:- I am late for my class

- How are they doing?

Answer:- They are doing well

Exercise

- What are you ……………...…….?

- Where are they ………………?

- When are you ………………..…?

- Why are they ………………...…?

- How are they …………………?

Chapter 2

Was,were – we use this to talk about emotion or action in the past which was continuous

Use "was" with I/he/she/it

Use "were" with we/you/they

Adjective

I was+ adjective
He was+ adjective
She was+ adjective
It was+ adjective

We were+ adjective
You were+ adjective
They were+ adjective

Examples

- I was tired yesterday
- He was late for class
- She was angry with him
- It was expensive
- We were ready for the class
- You were crazy
- They were awesome

Exercise

- I was ……………………..
- He was …………………..
- She was …………………..
- It was ……………………..
- We were …………………..
- You were …………………..
- They were …………………..

Verb + ing

I was+ verb-ing
He was+ verb-ing
She was+ verb-ing
It was+ verb-ing

We were+ verb-ing
You were+ verb-ing
They were+ verb-ing

Examples

- I was watching football
- He was abusing the old man
- She was supporting them
- It was sinking
- We were waiting for you
- You were praising him
- They were organizing a party

Exercise

- I was ....

- He was ....

- She was ....

- It was ....

- We were..................

- You were ....

- They were...............

Preposition

I was + preposition + noun
He was+ preposition + noun
She was+ preposition + noun
It was+ preposition + noun

We were+ preposition + noun
You were+ preposition + noun
They were+ preposition + noun

Examples

- I was at home

- He was in class

- It was in the cup

- We were at the bus stop

- They were in the office

Exercise

- I was ………………………..

- He was …………………….

- It was ………………………..

- We were …………………..

- They were …………………….

Noun

I was+ noun (job)
He was + noun (job)
She was+ noun (job)

We were+ nouns (job)
You were+ noun/s (job)
They were+ noun (job)

Examples

- I was a teacher

- He was a builder

- We were painters

- You were a good salesman

Exercise

- I was ……………………

- He was …………………..

- We were …………………

- You were …………………

- They were ………………..

Negative

Adjective

I was not = I wasn't

He was not = he wasn't

She was not = she wasn't

We were not = we weren't

You were not = we weren't

They were not = they weren't

I was not + adjective
He was not + adjective
She was not + adjective
It was not + adjective
We were not + adjective
You were not + adjective
They were not + adjective
Examples

- I was not tired

- He was not faithful

- She wasn't upset

- It wasn't spicy

- We weren't excited

- You weren't interested

- They weren't helpful

29

Exercise

- I was not ....
- He was not ....
- She wasn't ....
- It wasn't ....
- We weren't ....
- You weren't ....
- They weren't ....

Verb + ing

I was not + verb-ing
He was not + verb-ing
She was not + verb-ing
It was not + verb-ing
We were not + verb-ing
You were not + verb-ing
They were not + verb-ing

Examples

- I was not shouting
- He was not making tea
- She was not writing
- It was not raining
- We were not playing
- You were not listening
- They were not working

Exercise

- I was not ....

- He was not ....

- She was not ....

- It was not ....

- We were not ....

- You were not ....

- They were not ....

Preposition

I was not + preposition + noun
He was not + preposition + noun
She was not + preposition + noun
It was not + preposition + noun

We were not + preposition + noun
You were not + preposition + noun
They were not + preposition + noun

Examples

- I was not at home

- He was not in class

- It was not in the cup

- We were not at the bus stop

- They were not in the office

Exercise

- I was not ....

- He was not ....

- It was not ....

- We were not ....

- They were not ....

NOUN

I was not+ noun (job)
He was not + noun (job)
She was not + noun (job)
We were not + nouns (job)
You were not + noun/s (job)
They were not + noun (job)

Examples

- I was not a teacher

- He was not a builder

- We were not painters

- You were not a good salesman

Exercise

- I was not ....

- He was not ....

- We were not ....

- You were not ....

- They were not ....

Questions

Adjective

Was I + adjective?
Was he + adjective?
Was she + adjective?
Was it + adjective?
Were we + adjective?
Were you + adjective?
Were they + adjective?

Examples

- Was I bold?

Answer:- You were bold/You were not bold

- Was he helpful?

Answer:- He was helpful/ He was not helpful

- Was she pretty?

Answer:- She was pretty /She was not pretty

- Were you excited about the trip?

Answer:- I was excited about the trip/I was not excited about the trip

- Were they happy to see me?

Answer:- they were happy to see you/ They were not happy to see you.

Exercise

- Was I ………………..…?

- Was he ……………...……?

- Was she ……………..……?

- Were you …………………?

- Were they …………………?

Verb

Was I + verb-ing?
Was he + verb-ing?
Was she + verb-ing?
Was it + verb-ing?
Were we + verb-ing?
Were you + verb-ing?
Were they + verb-ing?
Examples

- Was he playing with this?

Answer:- He was playing with this/ He was not playing with this

- Was she irritating him?

Answer:- She was irritating him /She was not irritating him

- Were you waiting for me?

Answer:- I was waiting for you /I was not waiting for you

- Were they stealing from him?

Answer:- They were stealing from him/They were not stealing from him

Exercise

- Was he ……………...……?

- Was she ……………..……?

- Were you ……………….……?

- Were they ……………….……?

Preposition

Was he + preposition+ noun?
Was she+ preposition+ noun?
Was it+ preposition+ noun?
Were we+ preposition+ noun?
Were you + preposition+ noun?
 Were they+ preposition+ noun?

Examples

- Was he at home?

Answer :- He was at home/He was not at home

- Was she in the class?

Answer:- She was in the class/She was not in the class

- Were you in trouble?

Answer:- I was in trouble/I was not in trouble

Exercise

- Was he ………………....…?

- Was she ………………..……?

- Were you …………………?

- Were they …………………?

Noun

Was he + noun (job)?
Was she+ noun (job)?
Were you+ noun/s (job)?
Were they+ noun (job)?

Examples

- Was he a builder?

- Were they painters?

- Were you a good salesman?

Exercise

- Was he.......................?

- Were you.....................?

- Were they ....?

Wh- Questions

Verb

What was he/she + verb-ing?

Where was he/she + verb-ing?

When was he/she + verb-ing?

Why was he/she + verb-ing?

How was he/she + verb-ing?

Examples

- What was he doing?

Answer:- He was washing his clothes

- Where was she teaching?

Answer:- She was teaching in Canada

- Why was he crying?

Answer:- He was sick

- How was she dancing?

Answer:- She was dancing well

Exercise

- What was he ....?
- Where was she ....?
- Why was he ....?
- How was he ....?

39

What were we/you/they + verb-ing?

Where were we/you/they + verb-ing?

When were we/you/they + verb-ing?

Why were we/you/they + verb-ing?

How were we/you/they + verb-ing?

Examples

- What were you giving her?

Answer:- I was helping her with some money

- Where were they staying?

Answer:- They were staying with their friends

- Why were you running?

Answer:- I was going to meet my friend

- How were they carrying the boxes?

Answer:- They were using a cart

Exercise

- What were you ....?
- Where were they ....?
- Why were you ....?
- How were they ....?

Chapter 3

Simple present – we use it to talk about actions that happens regularly or now

Example:- walk, like,eat,drink,study etc....

I + verb
We+ verb
You + verb
They + verb

Examples

- I like coke

- We prefer tea

- You study well

- They want water

Exercise

- I ....

- We ....

- You ....

- They ....

Negative

I do not (don't) + verb
We do not (don't) + verb
You do not (don't) + verb
They do not (don't) + verb

Examples

- I don't like this

- We don't believe that

- You don't listen to me

- They don't help us

Exercise

- I don't ……………………..

- We don't …………………..

- You don't …………………

- They don't …………………

Question

Do I + verb?
 Do we+ verb?
Do you + verb?
Do they + verb?

Examples

- Do you work here?

Answer:- I work here/ I don't work here

- Do they live here?

Answer:- They live here/They don't live here

- Do I annoy you?

Answer:- You annoy me/You don't annoy me

Exercise

- Do you ....?

- Do they ....?

- Do I ....?

Wh- Questions

What do we/you/they + verb?
Where do we/you/they + verb?
When do we/you/they + verb?
Why do we/you/they + verb?
How do we/you/they + verb?

Examples

- What do you want?

Answer:- I want a doughnut

- Where do they exercise?

Answer:- They exercise at the gym

- When do you get up ?

Answer:- I get up at 6 in the morning

- Why do you talk to him?

Answer:- He is my best friend (Sometimes we can use other tense sentences as answers)

- How do they get to school?

Answer:- They take bus

Exercise

- What do ………………...…….?
- Where do …………………….?
- When do ………………...…….?
- Why do …………………...…….?
- How do …………………...…….?

He/She/It

He + verb (s/es/ies)

She + verb (s/es/ies)

It+ verb (s/es/ies)

When we use he/she/it with simple form verbs we have to add s/es/ies to the end of the verb

Examples –

Eat = eats

Study = studies

Go = goes

Help = helps

verbs ending in	Add	Eg:-
e	s	likes
ie	s	lies
o	es	goes
sh/ch/tch/x/z/s	es	watches/kisses/fixes/pushes

Verbs ending with a consonant + y , change "y" to "ie" and add "s"
eg:- try - tries
imply - implies

For other verbs add "s"	
Work = works	
stay = stays	here it is a vowel + y
know = knows	
Dance = Dances	

Examples

- He likes ice cream

- She plays well

- It opens at 10 in the morning

Exercise

- He …………………..

- She …………………

- It ……………………

Negative

He does not + verb

She does not + verb

It does not + verb

In the negative we use does not /doesn't with simple verbs. Addition of s/es/ies is not done in the negative

Examples

- He doesn't support us

- She doesn't care about him

- It doesn't work properly

Exercise

- He …………………..

- She …………………

- It ……………………

Question

Does he+ verb?

Does she+ verb?

Does it + verb?

Examples

- Does he study here?

Answer:- He studies here/He doesn't study here

- Does she know you?

Answer:- She knows me/She doesn't know me

- Does it work?

Answer:- It works /It doesn't work

Exercise

- Does he ………………….?
- Does she …………………?
- Does it ……………………?

Wh- Questions

What does he/she + verb?
Where does he/she + verb?
When does he/she + verb?
Why does he/she + verb?
How does he/she + verb?

Examples

- What does he do in the morning?

Answer:- He goes to college

- Where does she get the money from?

Answer:- Her uncle sends money to her

- When does he get up?

Answer:- He gets up late

- Why does she go there?

Answer:- She goes to meet her friend

- How does he go to college?

Answer:- He takes a bus

Exercise

- What does he ....?
- Where does she ....?
- When does he ....?
- Why does she ....?
- How does he ....?

Chapter 4

Have

I have + noun
We have + noun
You have + noun
They have + noun

Examples

- I have a suggestion

- We have enough work

- You have a problem with him

- They have lots of products

Exercise

- I have ....

- We have ....

- You have ....

- They have ....

Negative

Do not = don't

I don't have + noun
We don't have + noun
You don't have + noun
They don't have + noun

Examples

I don't have any idea

We don't have work here

You don't have good friends

They don't have money

Exercise

I don't ....

We don't ....

You don't ....

They don't ....

Question

Do I have + noun?
Do we have + noun?
Do you have + noun?
Do they have + noun?

Examples

- Do I have a part in this ?

Answer:- you have a part in this /you don't have a part in this
- Do we have any problems there?

Answer:- we have problems there /we don't have any problems there
- Do you have anything to say?

Answer:- I have something to say/ I don't have anything to say
- Do they have permission?

Answer:- They have permission /they don't have permission

Exercise

- Do I have ………………....……?
- Do we have ……………..…….?
- Do you have …………….…….?
- Do they have …………….…….?

Has

He has + noun
She has + noun
It has + noun

Examples

- He has a big brother
- She has a little sister
- It has sugar

Exercise

- He has ....
- She has ....
- It has ....

Negative

Does not = doesn't

He doesn't have + noun
She doesn't have + noun
It doesn't have + noun

Examples

- He doesn't have a Ferrari
- She doesn't have a boyfriend
- It doesn't have sugar

Exercise

- He doesn't have ....

- She doesn't have ....

- It doesn't have ....

Chapter 5

Have got

I have got + noun
We have got + noun
You have got + noun
They have got + noun

Examples

- I've got a plan
- We've got money
- You've got a recommendation letter
- They've got a problem

Exercise

- I've got ....

- We've got ....

- You've got ....

- They've got ....

Question

Have I got + noun?
Have we got + noun?
Have you got + noun?
Have they got + noun?

Examples

- Have you got ketchup?

Answer:- I have /I don't have or I have got/ I haven't got

- Have they got books?

Answer:- They have/They don't have or They have got/They haven't got

Exercise

- Have you got ....?
- Have they got ....?
- Have we got ....?

Has got

He has got + noun
She has got + noun
It has got + noun
Examples

- He has got my books

- She has got his number

- It has got wifi

Exercise

- He has got ....
- She has got ....
- It has got ....

Question

Has he got + noun?
Has she got + noun?
Has it got + noun?

Examples

- Has he got a girlfriend ?

Answer:- He has /He doesn't have or He has got /He hasn't got
- Has it got Bluetooth?

Answer:- It has /It doesn't have or It has got/It hasn't got

Exercise

- Has he got ....?
- Has it got ....?

Chapter 6

Past simple – talks about a completed action in the past eg:- eat = ate, walk = walked, play = played, talk = talked

- **Add "d" to the verbs that end in a vowel and one or more consonants + e**

Ache	ached
bake	baked
blame	blamed
Care	cared
chase	chased
hate	hated
live	lived
raise	raised
slice	sliced
spare	spared
surprise	surprised
taste	tasted

- **If there is a single stressed vowel before the final consonant then double the final consonant and add "ed"**

Ban	banned
can	canned
sip	sipped
prefer	preferred
refer	referred

- **Verbs that end in a consonant and "y", change "y" to "I" and add "ed"**

This rule doesn't apply when a verb ends in a vowel and "y"

Apply	applied
bury	buried
dry	dried
carry	carried
fry	fried
marry	married
try	tried

Annoy	annoyed
destroy	destroyed
enjoy	enjoyed
obey	obeyed
play	played
pray	prayed
stay	stayed

- **Add "ed" to the base forms of all other regular verbs.**

- **What we have seen above are regular verbs. Now we will see irregular verbs and they don't have easy rules for forming the past tense as the regular verbs**

Arise	arose		come	came
awake	awoke		cut	cut
become	became		do	did
bet	bet		dream	dreamt
bind	bound		drink	drank
blow	blew		drive	drove
break	broke		eat	ate
bring	brought		fall	fell
build	built		fight	fought
Buy	Bought		fly	flew

forget	forgot
forgive	forgave
give	gave
go	went
have	had
keep	kept
know	knew

I+ verb (past tense)
We+ verb (past tense)
You + verb (past tense)
They+ verb (past tense)
He + verb (past tense)
She + verb (past tense)
It + verb (past tense)
Examples

- I called him yesterday

- We helped him a lot

- You told me that story

- They forgot my name

- He gave me a bad apple

- She understood the class

- It rained yesterday

Exercise

- I ....

- We ....

- You ....

- They ....

- He ....

- She ....

- It ....

Negative

I did not + verb (simple present)
We did not + verb (simple present)
You did not + verb (simple present)
They did not + verb (simple present)
He did not + verb (simple present)
She did not + verb (simple present)
It did not + verb (simple present)

did not = didn't

Examples

- I didn't tell him that
- We didn't meet him there
- You didn't call us
- They didn't feel comfortable
- He didn't eat anything
- She didn't speak a word
- It didn't open

Exercise

- I didn't ....

- We didn't ....

- You didn't ....

- They didn't ....

- He didn't ....

- She didn't ....

- It didn't ....

Question

Did I + verb(simple present)?
Did we+ verb(simple present)?
Did you + verb(simple present)?
Did they + verb(simple present)?
Did he + verb(simple present)?
Did she + verb(simple present)?
Did it + verb(simple present)?

Examples

- Did I tell you about Harry?

Answer:- You told me/ you didn't tell me

- Did we meet the right person?

Answer:- I think so /I don't know (sometimes we can use other tense sentences as answers)

- Did you understand the class?

Answer:- I understood/ I didn't understand a thing

- Did they agree with you?

Answer:- They agreed/ They disagreed

- Did he get married?

Answer:- He got married last month/He didn't get married

- Did she change the book?

Answer:- I think so /I don't know

Exercise

- Did I ....?
- Did we ....?
- Did you ....?
- Did they ....?
- Did he ....?
- Did she ....?
- Did it ....?

Wh- Questions

What did I/we/you/they/he/she/it + verb(simple present)?
Where did I/we/you/they/he/she/it + verb(simple present)?
When did I/we/you/they/he/she/it + verb(simple present)?
Why did I/we/you/they/he/she/it + verb(simple present)?
How did I/we/you/they/he/she/it + verb(simple present)?

Examples

- What did I forget?

Answer:- I think you forgot your books

- Where did he meet her?

Answer:- They met at the bus stop

- When did she tell you this?

Answer:- She told me this yesterday

- Why did she leave him?

Answer:- He cheated on her

- How did she come?

Answer:- She took a cab

Exercise

- What did I ....?
- Where did he ....?
- When did she ....?
- Why did she ....?
- How did she ....?

Chapter 7

Future

"will" is used for future tense but it is considered not as strong as "going to "

I will + verb
We will + verb
You will + verb
They will + verb
He will + verb
She will + verb
It will + verb

Examples

- I will encourage him
- We will make new plans
- You will get the money soon
- He will confuse us
- She will take care of him
- It will work well

Exercise

- I will…………………………
- We will ……………………..
- You will ……………………..
- He will ………………………
- She will ……………………..
- It will ………………………..

Negative

I will not + verb
We will not + verb
You will not + verb
They will not + verb
He will not + verb
She will not + verb
It will not + verb

Will not = won't
Examples

- I won't tell him anything

- We won't help him

- You won't understand this

- They won't have lunch here

- He won't share the details

- She won't blame you

Exercise

- I won't ....

- We won't ....

- You won't.......................

- They won't.......................

- He won't ....

- She won't ....

Question

Will I+ verb?
Will we+ verb?
Will you + verb?
Will they + verb?
Will he + verb?
Will she + verb?
Will it+ verb?

Examples

- Will I get my book today?

Answer:- I think you will get it today/ You won't get it today

- Will we make it there on time?

Answer:- We will make it on time/ we won't reach on time

- Will you help us?

Answer:- I will help you/I won't help you

- Will they play well ?

Answer:- They will play well/They won't play well

- Will he finish the work on time?

Answer:- He will finish on time/He won't finish on time

- Will she get married this year?

Answer:- She will get married this year/She won't get married this year

Exercise

- Will I ....?

- Will we ....?

- Will you.........................?

- Will they ....?

- Will he ....?

- Will she ....?

- Will it ....?

Wh- Questions

What will I/we/you/they/he/she + verb?
Where will I/we/you/they/he/she+ verb?
When will I/we/you/they/he/she + verb?
How will I/we/you/they/he/she + verb?

Examples

- What will I tell them?

Answer:- Tell them you will call later (informal way of answering)

- Where will they meet her?

Answer:- They will meet her at the airport

- When will she call?

Answer:- She will call today

- How will he come?

Answer:- He will come by bus

Exercise
- What will I ………………...…………?

- Where will they ………………………?

- When will she …………….....…………?

- How will he …………………....……?

Adjective

I will be + adjective
We will be + adjective
You will be + adjective
They will be + adjective
He will be + adjective
She will be + adjective
It will be + adjective

Examples

- I will be late for class
- We will be happy
- You will be proud
- They will be furious
- He will be tired
- She will be victorious
- It will be heavy
  Exercise
- I will be ....

- We will be ....

- You will be ....

- They will be ....

- He will be ....

- She will be ....

- It will be ....

Adjective- Negative

I will not be + adjective
We will not be + adjective
You will not be + adjective
They will not be + adjective
He will not be + adjective
She will not be + adjective
It will not be + adjective

Examples

- They won't be late

- He won't be jealous

- She won't be cruel

- It won't be expensive

Exercise

- They won't be ……………..

- He won't be ……………….

- She won't be ………………

- It won't be …………………

Preposition

I will be + preposition + Place
We will be + preposition + Place
You will be + preposition + Place
They will be + preposition + Place
He will be + preposition + Place
She will be + preposition + Place
It will be + preposition + Place

Examples

- I will be at home

- You will be in class

- He will be with her

- It will be in the box

Exercise

- I will be ………………...

- You will be ……………..

- He will be ………………

- It will be ……………….

Preposition –Negative

I will not be + preposition + noun
We will not be + preposition + noun
You will not be + preposition + noun
They will not be + preposition + noun
He will not be + preposition + noun
She will not be + preposition + noun
It will not be + preposition + noun

Examples

- He won't be on time

- They won't be at home

- She won't be in class

- It won't be in the shop

Exercise

- He won't be ....

- They won't be ....

- She won't be ....

- It won't be ....

Verb-Ing

I will be + verb-ing
We will be + verb-ing
You will be + verb-ing
They will be + verb-ing
He will be + verb-ing
She will be + verb-ing
It will be + verb-ing

Examples

- I will be coming there

- You will be helping her

- She will be getting her money soon

- He will be cooking lunch

Exercise

- I will be ………………..

- You will be ……………..

- She will be ……………..

- He will be ……………..

Chapter 8

Future – Going to

I am going to + verb

He is going to + verb
She is going to + verb
It is going to + verb

We are going to + verb
You are going to + verb
They are going to + verb

Examples

- I am going to help him
- She is going to call us
- He is going to call us
- We are going to go home
- You are going to get money
- They are going to wash clothes
  Exercise
- I am going to …………………..

- She is going to ………………..

- He is going to ……………...…..

- We are going to ………………..

- You are going to ……………...….

- They are going to ………………..

Negative

I am not going to + verb

He is not going to + verb
She is not going to + verb
It is not going to + verb

We are not going to + verb
You are not going to + verb
They are not going to + verb

Examples

- I am not going to tell you

- He isn't going to call

- We aren't going to miss

- They aren't going to rush

- It isn't going to rain

Exercise

- I am not going to ……………..

- He isn't going to ……………..

- We aren't going to ……………

- They aren't going to …………

- It isn't going to ………………

Question

Am I going to + verb?

Is he going to + verb?
Is she going to + verb?
Is It going to + verb?

Are we going to + verb?
Are you going to + verb?
Are they going to + verb?

Examples

- Is he going to marry her?

Answer:- He is going to marry her/He is not going to marry her

- Are you going to quit ?

Answer:- I am going to quit/I am not going to quit

- Are they going to fire him?

Answer:- they are going to fire him/they are not going to fire him

Exercise
- Is he going to ……………....?

- Are you going to ……………..?

- Are they going to ……………?

- Is she going to ………………..?

Wh- Questions

What is he/she going to + verb?
Where is he/she going to + verb?
When is he/she going to + verb?
Why is he/she going to + verb?
How is he/she going to + verb?

Examples

- What is he going to do?

Answer:- He is going to call the Manager

- Where is she going to practice ?

Answer:- She is going to practice at home

- When is he going to give an answer?

Answer:- He is going to answer soon

- Why is she going to meet him?

Answer:- She is going to discuss something

- How is he going to impress her?

Answer:- He is going to sing a song

Exercise

- What is he going to ....?
- Where is she going to ....?
- When is he going to ....?
- Why is she going to ....?
- Why is she going to ....?
- How is he going to ....?

What are we/you/they going to + verb?
Where are we/you/they going to + verb?
When are we/you/they going to + verb?
Why are we/you/they going to + verb?
How are we/you/they going to + verb?

Examples

- What are we going to have?

Answer:- we will have pizza (we can use sentences with "will" to give reply , it is considered as informal)

- Where are you going to go?

Answer:- I am going to go to Australia

- When are they going to build this?

Answer:- They are going to start work this month

- Why are you going to invest in this company?

Answer:- I am not going to invest

- How are they going to fix it?

Answer:- They are going to call someone

Exercise

- What are we going to ....?

- Where are they going to ....?

- When are you going to ....?

- Why are they going to ....?

- How are you going to ....?

Chapter 9

Should – used to indicate duty, probability, suggestion

I should + verb
We should + verb
You should + verb
They should + verb
He should + verb
She should + verb

Examples

- I should help him
- We should appreciate her
- They should listen to her
- You should buy this book
- He should respect her
- She should start teaching
  Exercise
- I should ……………..

- We should ………….

- They should …………

- You should …………

- He should …………..

- She should …………

Negative

I should not + verb
We should not + verb
You should not + verb
They should not + verb
He should not + verb
She should not + verb

Should not = shouldn't

Examples

I shouldn't encourage him
We shouldn't ask him
You shouldn't touch this
He shouldn't spoil his name
She shouldn't criticize them

Exercise

I shouldn't ....

We shouldn't ....

You shouldn't ....

He shouldn't ....

She shouldn't ....

Question

Should I + verb?
Should we + verb?
Should you + verb?
Should they + verb?
Should he + verb?
Should she + verb?

Examples

- Should I help him ?

Answer:- You should help him/You shouldn't help him

- Should we support her?

Answer:- We should support her/We shouldn't support her

- Should he participate in the competition ?

Answer:- He should participate/He shouldn't participate

- Should she take a loan?

Answer:- She should take a loan/She shouldn't take a loan

Exercise
- Should I ....?

- Should we ....?

- Should she ....?

- Should they ....?

Wh- Questions

What should I/we/you/they/he/she + verb?
Where should I/we/you/they/he/she + verb?
When should I/we/you/they/he/she + verb?
Why should I/we/you/they/he/she + verb?
How should I/we/you/they/he/she + verb?

Examples

- What should I buy?

Answer:- You should try the chocolates they have

- Where should we have lunch?

Answer:- We can go to McDonalds (this is a suggestion)

- When should he start cooking?

Answer:- He should start now

- Why should I eat this?

Answer:- It is good for you (not necessary to use the same tense or sentence structure to give an answer)

- How should they give the book?

Answer:- They should gift wrap it

Exercise

- What should I ………...?

- Where should he ……...?

- When should she ……...?

- Why should they ……...?

- How should we ………...?

Chapter 10

Must:- Used to indicate obligation,need to,compelled to

I must + verb
We must + verb
You must + verb
They must + verb
He must + verb
She must + verb

Examples

- I must develop a new app

- We must improve our language

- You must maintain your dignity

- They must decide quickly

- He must protect her

- She must avoid sweets

  Exercise
- I must ....

- We must ....

- You must ....

- They must ....

- He must ....

- She must ....

85

Negative

I must not + verb
We must not + verb
You must not + verb
They must not + verb
He must not + verb
She must not + verb

Must not = mustn't
Examples

- We mustn't include this in the list

- You mustn't forget the rules

- They mustn't harm the animals

- He mustn't spend all the money

- She mustn't lose faith

- It mustn't exceed the limit

Exercise

- We mustn't ....

- You mustn't ....

- They mustn't ....

- He mustn't ....

- She mustn't ....

- It mustn't ....

  ❖ **Questions with must are rarely used**

86

Chapter 11

Might - to express possibility

I might + verb
We might + verb
You might + verb
They might + verb
He might + verb
She might + verb

Examples

- I might get the visa
- We might represent our school
- You might get scholarship
- They might expand their business
- He might send some money
- She might settle down in Canada
- It might rain today
  Exercise
- I might ....
- We might ....
- You might ....
- They might ....
- He might ....
- She might ....
- It might ....

Negative

I might not + verb
We might not + verb
You might not + verb
They might not + verb
He might not + verb
She might not + verb

Examples

- I might not like it

- We might not close the deal

- You might not compete with him

- He might not qualify for the job

- She might not apologize

- It might not rain today

Exercise

- I might not ……………..

- We might not …………..

- You might not …………..

- He might not ……………

- She might not …………..

- It might not ……………..

Chapter 12

Can

I can+ verb
We can+ verb
You can+ verb
They can+ verb
He can+ verb
She can+ verb

Examples

- I can help you

- We can explore this place

- You can emphasize your point

- They can install the software

- He can extend his holidays

- She can teach them

Exercise

- I can ....

- We can ....

- You can ....

- They can ....

- He can ....

- She can ....

Negative

I cannot + verb
We cannot + verb
You cannot + verb
They cannot + verb
He cannot + verb
She cannot + verb

Examples

- Cannot = can't

- I can't understand this

- We can't convince him

- You can't allow this

- They can't change the subject now

- He can't teach Greek

- She can't concentrate in class

Exercise

- I can't ……………..

- We can't ……………

- You can't ……………

- They can't ……………

- He can't ………………

- She can't ……………..

Question

Can I + verb?
Can we+ verb?
Can you + verb?
Can they+ verb?
Can he + verb?
Can she + verb?

Examples

Can I take this ?
Answer:- Yes you can /No you can't
Can we start the class?
Answer:- We will start after sometime (we can use other tense sentences for replying)
Can you give me his number?
Answer:- I will send it t to you
Can they handle the business?
Answer:- I don't think so/ I think they can
Can he do this work?
Answer:- He can do it
Exercise
Can I ……………...…?

Can we ……………?

Can you ……………?

Can they ……………?

Can he ………………?

Wh-Questions

What can I/we/you/they/he/she/ + verb?
Where can I/we/you/they/he/she/ + verb?
When can I/we/you/they/he/she/ + verb?
How can I/we/you/they/he/she/ + verb?

Examples

- What can I give you?

Answer:- I want some cheese

- Where can we meet him?

Answer:- We can meet him at the gym

- When can we start our work?

Answer:- We will start next week

- How can they afford this?

Answer:- They have a lot of money

Exercise

- What can I ……………..……?

- Where can we ……………?

- When can he ……………..……?

- How can she ……………..……?

Couldn't

I couldn't + verb
We couldn't + verb
You couldn't + verb
They couldn't + verb
He couldn't + verb
She couldn't + verb

Could = past of can

Examples

- I couldn't meet him

- We couldn't cook lunch

- You couldn't improve your language

- They couldn't remember the lesson

- He couldn't believe her

- She couldn't reduce the price

  Exercise
- I couldn't ....

- We couldn't ....

- You couldn't ....

- They couldn't ....

- He couldn't ....

- She couldn't ....

93

Chapter 13

Have to/Has to - means obliged to (do something)/ necessary

I have to + verb
We have to + verb
You have to + verb
They have to + verb

Examples

- I have to call him

- We have to finish this today

- You have to release the payment

- They have to reduce the price

    Exercise
- I have to ………………………

- We have to ……………….

- You have to ………………..

- They have to ………………..

Negative

I don't have to + verb
We don't have to + verb
You don't have to + verb
They don't have to + verb

Examples

- I don't have to obey you

- We don't have to complain

- You don't have to depend on him

- They don't have to borrow money

  ### Exercise

- I don't have to …………..

- We don't have to …………

- You don't have to ………..

- They don't have to ………..

Question

Do I have to + verb?
Do we have to + verb?
Do you have to + verb?
Do they have to + verb?

Examples

- Do I have to study this?

Answer:- You have to / you don't have to
- Do we have to listen to this speech?

Answer:- You have to / You don't have to/It's up to you

Exercise
- Do I have to ....?

- Do we have to ....?

Has to

He has to + verb
She has to + verb

Examples

- He has to improve himself

- She has to cook

Exercise
- He has to ....

- She has to ....

Negative

He doesn't have to + verb
She doesn't have to + verb

Examples

- He doesn't have to recommend him

- She doesn't have to depend on anyone

  Exercise
- He doesn't have to …...........

- She doesn't have to ……….

Question

Does he have to + verb?
Does she have to + verb?

Examples

- Does he have to organize the party?

Answer:- He has to /He doesn't have to

- Does she have to translate this?

Answer:- She has to /She doesn't have to

  Exercise
- Does he have to …..?

- Does she have to …..?

Chapter 14

Have been - indicates something that has been happening over a period of time

I have been + Adjective + for/since + time

We have been + Adjective + for/since + time

You have been + Adjective + for/since + time

They have been + Adjective + for/since + time

- **For –to talk about duration of time eg:- for 10 years, for 5 minutes.**

- **Since- to talk about time when the action started**

Examples

- I have been married for 8 years

- We have been married since 2010

- They have been sick for a week

Exercise
- I have been ....
- We have been ....
- They have been ....

	for	since	
a week	five minutes	Wednesday	10 o' clock
a month	three hours	March	15-April
two years	a long time	2010	Ramadan

Verb

I have been + verb-ing+ for/since + time

We have been + verb-ing+ for/since + time

You have been + verb-ing+ for/since + time

They have been + verb-ing+ for/since + time

Examples

- I have been waiting for 10 minutes

- They have been working since 9:00 am

Exercise

- I have been.....................

- They have been...............

Has been

He has been + Adjective+ for/since + time

She has been + Adjective+ for/since + time

Examples

- He has been sick for 2 years

- She has been depressed since2015

Exercise

- He has been.....................

- She has been.....................

Verb

He has been + verb-ing+ for/since + time

She has been + verb-ing+ for/since + time

Examples

He has been complaining for 3 days

She has been teaching since 2015

Exercise

He has been.....................

She has been.....................

Chapter 15

How long have ...... been - asking duration of an action or duration of a condition/situation

How long have you been + verb –ing?
How long have we been + verb –ing?
How long have they been + verb –ing?

Examples

- How long have you been coaching?

Answer:- I have been coaching for 5 years

- How long have they been playing?

Answer:- They have been playing since 6:00 pm

Exercise

- How long have you been............?

- How long have they been............?

Adjective

How long have we been + adjective?
How long have you been + adjective?
How long have they been + adjective?
Examples

- How long have you been married?

Answer:- I have been married for 8 years

- How long have they been together?

Answer:- They have been together since 2010

Exercise

- How long have you been……………..?

- How long have they been……………..?

How long has...... been

Verb

How long has he been + verb –ing?
How long has she been + verb –ing?

Examples

- How long has he been swimming?

Answer:- He has been swimming for an hour

- How long has she been standing?

Answer:- She has been standing for 10 minutes

Exercise

- How long has he been...............?

- How long has she been.............?

Adjective

How long has he been + adjective?
How long has she been + adjective?

Examples

- How long has he been addicted to smoking?

Answer:- He has been smoking for years

- How long has she been jobless?

Answer:- She has been jobless since 2015

Exercise

- How long has he been.................?

- How long has she been................?

Chapter 16

A lot of

I verb + a lot of + noun
We verb + a lot of + noun
You verb + a lot of + noun
They verb + a lot of + noun

- **When you use noun here, use plural of the countable noun**
  Eg- books, bikes etc..
- **For uncountable nouns there are no plural forms**

Examples

- I read a lot of books

- We drink a lot of water

- You know a lot of people

- They make a lot of noise

Exercise

- I ………………………..

- We………………………

- You ……………………..

- They ……………………..

Negative

I don't +verb + a lot of + noun
We don't +verb + a lot of + noun
You don't +verb + a lot of + noun
They don't +verb + a lot of + noun

Examples

- I don't know a lot of people

- We don't read a lot of books

- They don't allow a lot of visitors

- You don't attend a lot of classes

Exercise

- I don't ………………………..

- We don't …………………..

- They don't …………………

- You don't …………………..

Question

Do I + verb + a lot of + noun?
Do we + verb + a lot of + noun?
Do you verb + a lot of + noun?
Do they + verb + a lot of + noun?

Examples

- Do you read a lot of books?

Answer:- I read a lot of books/I don't read a lot

- Do they have a lot of friends?

Answer:- They have a lot of friends/ They don't have a lot of friends

Exercise

- Do you…………….…..?

- Do they ………………..?

He/she

He+verb(s/es/ies) + a lot of + noun

She+verb(s/es/ies) + a lot of + noun

Examples

- He reads a lot of books

- She makes a lot of dishes

Exercise

- He ………………..

- She ………………..

Negative

He doesn't + Verb + a lot of + noun

She doesn't + Verb + a lot of + noun

Examples

- He doesn't eat a lot of food

- She doesn't buy a lot of things

Exercise

- He doesn't ………………..

- She doesn't ………………..

Questions

Does he + verb + a lot of + noun?
Does he + verb + a lot of + noun?

Examples

Does he eat a lot of cookies?

Answer:- He eats a lot/ He doesn't eat a lot

Does she write a lot of articles?

Answer:- She writes a lot of articles/She doesn't writes a lot of articles

Exercise

Does he ....?

Does she ....?

Chapter 17

Have enough

I have enough+ noun
We have enough+ noun
You have enough+ noun
They have enough+ noun

- **When you use noun here use plural of the countable noun**
  Eg- books, bikes etc..
- **For uncountable nouns there are no plural forms**

Examples

- I have enough books

- We have enough money

- They have enough students

Exercise

- I have enough ....

- We have enough ....

- They have enough ....

Negative

I don't have enough+ noun
We don't have enough+ noun
You don't have enough+ noun
They don't have enough+ noun

Examples

- We don't have enough time
- They don't have enough food
- You don't have enough experience

Exercise

- We don't have enough …................
- They don't have enough …..............
- You don't have enough …..............

Question

Do I have enough + noun?
Do we have enough + noun?
Do you have enough + noun?
Do they have enough + noun?

Examples

- Do you have enough money?

Answer:- I have enough money/I don't have enough money

- Do they have enough raw materials?

Answer:- They have enough materials/They don't have enough

- Do you have enough..............?

- Do they have enough..............?

Didn't have enough

I didn't have enough + noun
We didn't have enough + noun
You didn't have enough + noun
They didn't have enough + noun
He didn't have enough + noun
She didn't have enough + noun

Examples

- They didn't have enough food

- We didn't have enough students

- He didn't have enough time to finish

- She didn't have enough soup

Exercise

- They didn't have enough ....

- We didn't have enough ....

- He didn't have enough ....

- She didn't have enough ....

Question

Did I have enough + noun?
Did we have enough + noun?
Did you have enough + noun?
Did they have enough + noun?
Did he have enough + noun?
Did she have enough + noun?

Examples

- Did they have enough support?

Answer:- They had good support/They didn't have enough support

- Did you have enough water?

Answer:- I had enough/I didn't have enough

Exercise

- Did they have enough ....?
- Did you have enough ....?

Has enough

He has enough + noun
She has enough + noun

Examples

- He has enough friends

- She has enough help

Exercise

- He has enough...........

- She has enough..........

Negative

He doesn't have enough + noun
She doesn't have enough + noun

Examples

- He doesn't have enough money

- She doesn't have enough students

Exercise

- He doesn't have enough..............

- She doesn't have enough..............

Question

Does he have enough+ noun?
Does she have enough+ noun?

Examples

- Does he have enough water?

Answer:- He has enough water/he doesn't have enough

- Does she have enough flour?

Answer:- She has enough flour/She doesn't have

Exercise

- Does he have enough.............?

- Does she have enough............?

Chapter 18

Always/Never/Often

I always/never/often + verb
We always/never/often + verb
You always/never/often + verb
They always/never/often + verb

Examples

- I always remind him to call

- We never buy any illegal things

- They often meet at KFC

Exercise

- I always.................

- We never ....

Question

Do I always/never/often + verb?
Do we always/never/often + verb?
Do you always/never/often + verb?
Do they always/never/often + verb?

Examples

- Do you always exercise in the morning?

Answer:- I always exercise in the morning/I often exercise in the morning/ I never exercise in the morning

- Do they never help you?

Answer:- They never help me/They often help me

Exercise

- Do you always...................?
- Do they never...................?

He/She/It

He always/never/often + verb(s/es/ies)
She always/never/often + verb(s/es/ies)
It always/never/often + verb(s/es/ies)

Examples

- He always gives an excuse

- She never comes on time

- It often falls down

Exercise

- He always ……………

- She never ……………

- It often ………………

Question

Does he always/never/often+verb?
Does she always/never/often+verb?
Does she always/never/often+verb?

Examples

- Does he always irritate you?

Answer:- He always irritates me

- Does she often call you?

Answer:- She calls me often

Exercise

- Does he always ....?

- Does she often ....?

Adjective

I am always/never/often + adjective

He is always/never/often + adjective
She is always/never/often + adjective
It is always/never/often + adjective

We are always/never/often + adjective
You are always/never/often + adjective
They are always/never/often + adjective

Examples

- He is always busy with his work
- We are never late for class

Exercise

- He is always ....
- We are never ....

Question

Am I always/never/often + adjective?

Is he always/never/often + adjective?
Is she always/never/often + adjective?
Is it always/never/often + adjective?

Are we always/never/often + adjective?
Are you always/never/often + adjective?
Are they always/never/often + adjective?

Examples

- Is he always fussy?

Answer:- He is always fussy

- Are they never late for class?

Answer:- They are never late for class

Exercise

- Is he always ………………?

- Are they never ……………?

Will

I will always/never/often + verb
We will always/never/often + verb
You will always/never/often + verb
They will always/never/often + verb
He will always/never/often + verb
She will always/never/often + verb

Examples

- I will always remember you

- They will never forget you

- She will never marry him

Exercise

- I will always ....

- They will never ....

- She will never ....

Chapter 19

Still

I still + verb
We still + verb
You still + verb
They still + verb

Examples

- I still remember that

- They still complain about it

Exercise

- You still ………….

- They still ………….

He/She/It

He still + verb(s/es/ies)
She still + verb(s/es/ies)

Examples

- He still smokes

- She still cares for him

Exercise

- He still …………..

- She still ………….

Chapter 20

Already

I already + verb(past tense)
We already + verb(past tense)
You already + verb(past tense)
They already + verb(past tense)
He already + verb(past tense)
She already + verb(past tense)

Examples

- I already told him the answer

- You already gave him the money

- He already bought a car

- She already broke up with him

Exercise

- I already ……………

- You already …………

- He already …………..

- She already ………….

Chapter 21

Afraid of

I am afraid of + Noun

He is afraid of + Noun
She is afraid of + Noun
It is afraid of + Noun

We are afraid of + Noun
You are afraid of + Noun
They are afraid of + Noun

Use uncountable nouns & plural countable nouns

Examples

- I am afraid of cats

- She is afraid of spiders

- They are afraid of darkness

Exercise

- I am afraid of ………….

- She is afraid of ………...

- They are afraid of ………

Question

Is he afraid of + noun?
Is she afraid of + noun?
Is it afraid of + noun?

Are we afraid of + noun?
Are you afraid of + noun?
Are they afraid of + noun?

Examples

- Is he afraid of bugs?

Answer:- He is /He isn't

- Is she afraid of ants?

Answer:- She is /She isn't

Exercise

- Is he afraid of ....?

- Is she afraid of ....?

Chapter 22

Scared to

I am scared to + verb
He is scared to + verb
She is scared to + verb
It is scared to + verb
We are scared to + verb
You are scared to + verb
They are scared to + verb

Examples

- He is scared to talk to her
- You are scared to catch the snake
- They are scared to meet her

Exercise

- He is scared to ....
- You are scared to ....
- They are scared to ....

127

Question

Is he scared to + verb?
Is she scared to + verb?
Is it scared to + verb?
Are we scared to + verb?
Are you scared to + verb?
Are they scared to + verb?

Examples

- Is he scared to go there?

Answer:- He is /He's not

- Are you scared to talk to her?

Answer:- I am /I am not

Exercise

- Is he scared to ……………..…?

- Are you scared to …………..?

Chapter 23

Able to

I am able to + verb

He is able to + verb
She is able to + verb
It is able to + verb

We are able to + verb
You are able to + verb
They are able to + verb

Examples

He is able to understand this

She is able to help him

Exercise

He is able to ………….

She is able to …………

Chapter 24

Interested in

I am interested in + noun

He is interested in + noun
She is interested in + noun
It is interested in + noun

We are interested in + noun
You are interested in + noun
They are interested in + noun

Examples

- He is interested in her

- She is interested in baseball

- They are interested in football

Exercise

- He is interested in …………

- She is interested in …………

- They are interested in ………

Chapter 25

Happy to

I am happy to + verb
He is happy to + verb
She is happy to + verb
It is happy to + verb
We are happy to + verb
You are happy to + verb
They are happy to + verb

Examples

- I am happy to meet you
- She is happy to teach
- We are happy to help you

Exercise

- I am happy to …………..
- She is happy to …………
- We are happy to ………..

Negative

I am not happy to + verb

He isn't happy to + verb
She isn't happy to + verb
It isn't happy to + verb

We aren't happy to + verb
You aren't happy to + verb
They aren't happy to + verb

Examples

- We aren't happy to accept this
- They aren't happy to meet him
- He isn't happy to see her

Exercise

- We aren't happy to ....

- They aren't happy to ....

- He isn't happy to ....

Question

Is he happy to + verb?
Is she happy to + verb?
Is it happy to + verb?

Are we happy to + verb?
Are you happy to + verb?
Are they happy to + verb?

Examples

- Is she happy to see me?

Answer:- she is/she isn't

- Are they happy to study here?

Answer:- They are /They aren't

Exercise

- Is she happy to ....?

- Are they happy to ....?

Chapter 26

Was about to

I was about to + verb
He was about to + verb
She was about to + verb
It was about to + verb

We were about to + verb
You were about to + verb
They were about to + verb

Examples

- I was about to call you

- He was about to marry her

- We were about to come there

- They were about to win

Exercise

- I was about to ……………………..

- He was about to…………………….

- We were about to …………………,,,

- They were about to ………………..

Chapter 27

Trying to

I am trying to + verb
He is trying to + verb
She is trying to + verb
It is trying to + verb
We are trying to + verb
You are trying to + verb
They are trying to + verb

Examples

- I am trying to start a new business
- We are trying to go to Canada

Exercise

- I am trying to ………………..
- We are trying to …………….

Question

- Is he trying to + verb?
- Is she trying to + verb?
- Is it trying to + verb?
- Are we trying to + verb?
- Are you trying to + verb?
- Are they trying to + verb?

Examples
- Is he trying to touch the ball?

Answer:- He is trying to kick the ball
- Are you trying to cheat her?

Answer:- I am not trying to cheat her
Exercise

- Is he trying to ....?

- Are you trying to ....?

Chapter 28

Turn to

It is my turn to + verb
It is our turn to + verb
It is your turn to + verb
It is his turn to + verb
It is her turn to + verb
It is their turn to + verb

Examples

- It is my turn to speak

- It is your turn to pay

- It is their turn to play

- It is our turn to swim

Exercise

- It is my turn to ……………

- It is your turn to ………….

- It is their turn to ………….

- It is our turn to …………...

Question

Is it my turn to + verb?
Is it our turn to + verb?
Is it your turn to + verb?
Is it his turn to + verb?
Is it her turn to + verb?
Is it their turn to + verb?

Examples

- Is it my turn to cook ?

- Answer:- It is/It isn't

- Is it your turn to pay?

- Answer:- It is /It isn't

Exercise

- Is it my turn to ....?

- Is it your turn to ....?

Chapter 29

Find it difficult to

I find it difficult to + verb
We find it difficult to + verb
You find it difficult to + verb
They find it difficult to + verb

Examples

- I find it difficult to believe him

- We find it difficult to adjust

Exercise

- I find it difficult to …………..

- We find it difficult to ………..

He/She

He finds it difficult to + verb

She finds it difficult to + verb

Examples

- He finds it difficult to cook
- She finds it difficult to manage the company

Exercise

- He finds it difficult to …………………………..

- She finds it difficult to ………………………

Question

Do I find it difficult to + verb?
Do we find it difficult to + verb?
Do you find it difficult to + verb?
Do they find it difficult to + verb?

Examples

- Do you find it difficult to play?

Answer:- Yes, I do/No I don't

- Do they find it difficult to understand the class?

Answer:- They understand the class/They find it difficult to understand

Exercise

- Do you find it difficult to ………..?

- Do they find it difficult to ………..?

He/She

Does he find it difficult to + verb?
Does she find it difficult to + verb?

Examples

- Does he find it difficult to walk ?

Answer:- He can walk/ he finds it difficult to walk

- Does she find it difficult to come here?

Answer:- She finds it difficult to come here

Exercise

- Does he find it difficult to …………?

- Does she find it difficult to …………?

Chapter 30

Supposed to

I am supposed to + verb
He is supposed to + verb
She is supposed to + verb
It is supposed to + verb
We are supposed to + verb
You are supposed to + verb
They are supposed to + verb

Examples

- He is supposed to attend the meeting
- She is supposed to cook lunch
- They are supposed to give us money

Exercise

- He is supposed to …………………………….
- She is supposed to …………………………..
- They are supposed to ………………………..

Question

Is he supposed to + verb?
Is she supposed to + verb?
Is it supposed to + verb?

Are we supposed to + verb?
Are you supposed to + verb?
Are they supposed to + verb?

Examples

- Are you supposed to run this business?

Answer:- Yes I am /No I am not

- Is he supposed to call her

Answer:- He is not supposed to call her

Exercise

- Are you supposed to ………….……?
- Is he supposed to ……………………?

Chapter 31

Dying to

I am dying to + verb

He is dying to + verb
She is dying to + verb

We are dying to + verb
You are dying to + verb
They are dying to + verb

Examples

- I am dying to meet her

- He is dying to move to a bigger house

- We are dying to expand our business

Exercise

- I am dying to ……………..

- He is dying to ……………..

- We are dying to ………….

Chapter 32

Excited to

I am excited to + verb

He is excited to + verb
She is excited to + verb
It is excited to + verb

We are excited to + verb
You are excited to + verb
They are excited to + verb

Examples

- I am excited to meet him

- We are excited to go there

Exercise

- I am excited to ....

- We are excited to ....

Chapter 33

Prepositions with Days/Months/Time/Season

	Monday
	Tuesday
	Wednesday
on	Thursday
	Friday
	Saturday
	Sunday
At	The weekend

- I met him on Monday
- We will meet on Friday

	Monday	
	Tuesday	morning
	Wednesday	afternoon
On	Thursday	evening
	Friday	night
	Saturday	
	Sunday	

- I met him on Monday morning
- We will meet on Friday night

In	the morning
at	Noon
In	the afternoon
In	the evening
at	night
at	midnight

- We have class in the morning
- She was in class at noon

	January
	February
	March
	April
in	May
	June
	July
	August
	September
	October
	November
	December

- Our classes will start in June
- She got married in July
- He will get engaged in May

	Summer
in	Winter
	Autumn
	Spring

- We have holidays in summer
- We will go to Alaska in winter

In	1995
	2010

- He was born in 1995
- He will release his new book in 2020

Chapter 34

Collocations - a collocation is two or more words that go together naturally

- We can use them with present, past or future tense

	Bath
	Drink
	A good time
	A hair cut
Have	A holiday
	A problem
	A relationship
	Rest
	Lunch
	Sympathy

- We will have a drink
- I had a problem yesterday

	Business
	Nothing
	Someone a favour
	The cooking
Do	The housework
	The shopping
	The washing up
	Homework
	One's best
	The dishes

- I can't do business with him
- She did all the cooking

	A difference
	A mess
	A mistake
	A noise
Make	An effort
	Furniture
	Money
	Progress
	Room
	Trouble

- He will make a mess
- Will she make money there?

	A break
	A chance
	A look
	A rest
Take	A seat
	A taxi
	An exam
	Notes
	Shower
	Class

- I want to take a break
- We don't want to take a chance
- He will take a look at your work

	A habit
	A promise
	A window
Break	Someone's heart
	The ice
	The law
	The Rules

- It is difficult to break a habit
- I never break a promise
- He broke her heart

	A ball
	A bus
	A chill
Catch	The flu
	Someone red handed
	Someone's attention

- I think I caught the flu
- She caught him red handed

	A fine
	Attention
	By cash
Pay	By card
	Someone a visit
	The bill

- He is not ready to pay the fine
- I like to pay by card
- We will pay him a visit

	Energy
	Money
	One's strength
Save	Someone a seat
	Someone's life
	Sth to the pen drive
	Space
	Time

- We need to save money
- He knows how to save time

	A diary
	A promise
	A secret
Keep	Calm
	In touch
	Quiet
	The change

- Can you keep a secret?
- You need to keep calm
- We will keep in touch

	Close
	Direct
	Early/late
Come	First/last
	On time
	Prepared
	To a decision
	To an agreement

- I am trying to come close
- He came early to class
- She came first

		Abroad
		Bad
		Bald
		Bankrupt
		Blind
		Crazy
		Deaf
		Fishing
Go		Mad
		Missing
		On foot
		Online
		Out of business
		To war
		Home

- The fruits are going bad
- He went bankrupt
- He will go crazy

	A job
	A shock
	Angry
	Divorced
	Drunk
	Scared
	Home
Get	Lost
	Married
	Permission
	Pregnant
	Ready
	Started
	The message
	Upset
	Worried

- He gets angry for no reason
- They got divorced
- She will get married in June

Chapter 35

Used to – habitual or accustomed actions/states taking place in the past but not continuing into the present

I used to + verb
We used to + verb
You used to + verb
They used to + verb
He used to + verb
She used to + verb

Examples

- I used to work here

- We used to study together

- They used to help us

- He used to talk to her

- She used to go out with him

Exercise

- I used to ………………….

- We used to …………………

- They used to ………………..

- He used to …………………..

- She used to …………………

Printed in Great Britain
by Amazon

45104240R00093